MW01288649

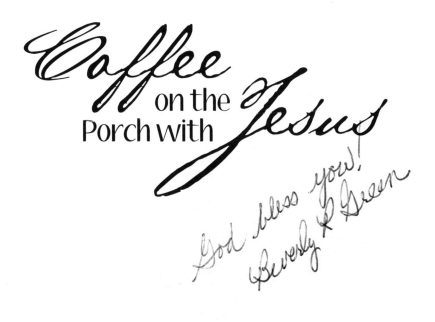

Coffee on the Porch with Jesus

God bless you!
Beverly R Green

BEVERLY R. GREEN

WESTBOW
P R E S S®
A DIVISION OF THOMAS NELSON
& ZONDERVAN

Copyright © 2016 Beverly R. Green.

All rights reserved. No part of this book may be used or reproduced by
any means, graphic, electronic, or mechanical, including photocopying,
recording, taping or by any information storage retrieval system
without the written permission of the author except in the case of
brief quotations embodied in critical articles and reviews.

WestBow Press books may be ordered through booksellers or by contacting:

WestBow Press
A Division of Thomas Nelson & Zondervan
1663 Liberty Drive
Bloomington, IN 47403
www.westbowpress.com
1 (866) 928-1240

Because of the dynamic nature of the Internet, any web addresses or
links contained in this book may have changed since publication and
may no longer be valid. The views expressed in this work are solely those
of the author and do not necessarily reflect the views of the publisher,
and the publisher hereby disclaims any responsibility for them.

Any people depicted in stock imagery provided by Thinkstock are models,
and such images are being used for illustrative purposes only.
Certain stock imagery © Thinkstock.

Scriptures taken from the Holy Bible, New International Version®, NIV®.
Copyright © 1973, 1978, 1984, 2011 by Biblica, Inc.™ Used by permission
of Zondervan. All rights reserved worldwide. www.zondervan.com The
"NIV" and "New International Version" are trademarks registered in
the United States Patent and Trademark Office by Biblica, Inc.™

Scripture quotations marked (KJV) taken from the King James Version.

ISBN: 978-1-5127-6004-0 (sc)
ISBN: 978-1-5127-6003-3 (hc)
ISBN: 978-1-5127-6005-7 (e)

Library of Congress Control Number: 2016916603

Print information available on the last page.

WestBow Press rev. date: 10/14/2016

Many thanks and much love to my brother, Dr. Edward L. Risden, who has always inspired my teaching and encouraged my writing.

Very special thanks and much love to my husband, Martine Green, who believed in me and my dream enough to make this book a reality.

★ ★ ★ ★ ★ ★ ★ ★

Coffee on the Porch with Jesus *is dedicated to Jorja, Penni and Risden. May you always know your Grammy's faith and how very much you are loved.*

Contents

A Walk in the Garden

The Hard Stuff

Before I Go...

Introduction

I love my front porch. It's one of the greatest places in the house. There are flowers, a fairy garden, bird-feeders, candles, comfortable furniture, and a nice view across a creek to a hillside with huge trees. I enjoy sitting out there, rain or shine, and I enjoy having company come over and sit with me as we drink a cup of coffee or a glass of iced tea and indulge in a leisurely conversation that usually unfolds something like this: a welcome and acknowledgement of the value of my guest, news about the family and work, then perhaps a walk in the garden to see what's growing there. After that, we might discuss serious topics, concerns, hurts, or problems. Finally, we part with words of encouragement and a promise to "do this again soon." Although I am not an extrovert, I am a very social being, and I love those long, thoughtful conversations. As an English teacher, words are my passion, and foundational to my work as well as to my recreation.

The God of the heavens and the earth is also a social being. He demonstrated that from the very beginning of time. When he decided to create the universe, he chose words as his medium. God *spoke* everything into existence. He created man, and allowed him to use words creatively, too. "He brought [all the beasts of the field and all the birds of the air] to the man to see what he would name them; and whatever the man called each living creature, that was its name" (Genesis 2:19b NIV). Humankind increased as God created woman for man, and the man named his wife Eve (Genesis 3:20a). People began to populate the world, social beings created in God's image and likeness and endowed with the power of words.

Of course, words got them into trouble in the Garden of Eden, at the Tower of Babel, and, it seems, ever since.

Fast forward to the New Testament, and the idea of the power and presence of the word remains. "In the beginning was the Word, and the Word was with God, and the Word was God" (John 1:1). The living Christ, the "Word made flesh," came to repair the relationship between God and man.

It's all about relationship. Unbelievable as it may be, our loving God wants that same relationship, communion and conversation with each one of us as he enjoyed with Adam and Eve before the fall, and our own spirits long for that relationship, communion and conversation with him. If you are a lover of written or spoken words, it is the God-likeness in you; it is you created in God's image with a divine gift. He desires communication and has told us over and over to come before him with our prayers and petitions and thanksgiving. We talk, he listens. We also need to accustom ourselves to listen and to allow him to answer.

My porch is where I listen best. Jesus is always there with me, but I wonder from time to time what it would be like if he were to come in the flesh, to sit down and have a cup of coffee with me there. How would that conversation go?

Let's Talk

1. Make Noise

As Christians we have a responsibility—to make noise for the kingdom of God! We have all heard the quote from Edmund Burke, "All that is necessary for the triumph of evil is that good men do nothing." Yet, the church in these days and dark times is often silent. As we search for significance as Christians, it is easy to become overwhelmed by the great amount of work that needs doing. We have the impression that "doing something" means doing something huge, yet scripture would lead us to believe that we should do good at every opportunity, regardless of the size of the act. Zechariah asks, "Who despises the day of small things?" The truth is that God can do a lot with a little. Remember the loaves and fishes? Gideon's army? Zacchaeus? The mustard seed?

Several years ago I lived on a peaceful country lane in Alabama. There also lived a flock (I suppose they are referred to as a flock) of guineas that made its way very loudly up the lane in single file at the same time each morning and returned at the same time each afternoon. It was miraculous! One could set the clock by those boisterous birds. In fact, it was their very volume that attracted my attention, for they could be heard squawking above a running air conditioner, television, or radio, with the windows and doors closed tight.

On one particular morning I looked out to find that my cat was separating one small guinea from the rest of the flock, smiling and licking his lips. The single small guinea looked like a goner, but the rest of the flock began to turn back and up into the yard, slowly surrounding and circling my cat and the little guinea. They didn't peck or flap their wings; they just paraded around in a single-file circle and made a lot of noise. None of those guineas alone would have been a match for my cat, but as a loud group they were so threatening that my cat backed up against a tree. The little guinea rejoined the flock, and they headed back on their course.

I think the church is a lot like those guineas. Our enemy comes "like a roaring lion seeking whom he may devour," but when we are part of a group that is making a lot of noise for the kingdom of God, he has to back up. We may not be too intimidating alone, but in a group we are mighty. In fact, God by our side makes even just one of us the majority.

That flock could have gone on, leaving the little guinea behind to suffer his fate, but they didn't—they made noise. We need to make noise on behalf of one another and the kingdom every day. First Corinthians tells us that God has "chosen the foolish things of this world to confound the wise," and we are exhorted in Galatians 6:10 to "do good to all people, especially the family of believers." That may put us in the spotlight from time to time, but most often we'll just be watching out for one another and trusting in our great, big brother who has already overcome the world.

Lord, help me to make joyful, useful noise today! Amen.

2. Plan A

How quickly did the first man mess things up with God! For goodness sake, God had just created him in Genesis 1:27, and by Genesis 3:23, God had to evict him! Then by Genesis 6:6, God was grieved and full of regret that he had ever created humans at all. Of the whole Bible, that's only 117 verses out of over 31,000 from creation to total depravity and wickedness—less than four pages in most Bibles!

Honestly, we really don't have an accurate concept of the time that elapsed between those events, but it obviously didn't take long for our sinful nature to surface. One of the saddest parts is that Adam and Eve, and even their children, really understood being in the *presence* of God. God actually walked with them in the beautiful garden (Genesis 3:8), and they fellowshipped together. The words of Cain after his great sin are heart-wrenching: "My punishment is more than I can bear. Today you are driving me from the land, and I will be hidden from your presence" (Genesis 4:13–14). To be hidden from his presence, the worst condition of all! It is worse than poverty, worse than sickness, worse than war, and worse than famine. Praise be to God that he was not without a plan to bring us back, and that it was *not* Plan B!

The sin of Adam and Eve did not take God by surprise. He was already assuring us in the midst of it all that he would "put enmity between you (the serpent) and the woman, and between your offspring and hers; he will crush your head, and you will strike his heel" (Genesis 3:15).

Satan continues to "strike the heel" of the body of Christ. One need only turn on the television or computer for five minutes, open the newspaper, or walk downtown to see it. Many experience it in some form on a day-to-day basis. "But Christ has indeed been raised from the dead, the first fruits of those who have fallen asleep. For since death came through a man, the resurrection from the dead comes also through a man. For as in Adam all will die, so in Christ will all be made alive" (1 Corinthians 15:20–22). The offspring of the serpent certainly struck, bruised, and pierced the heel of Christ, but that was not a death-dealing strike. The deathblow came as Christ crushed the head of his enemy and ours. Hallelujah! We are restored to right relationship and ushered back into the presence of God by the blood of the Lamb. What Adam broke, Jesus not only fixed, but redeemed. Now the Spirit of God not only walks with us in the cool of the day, but he abides within us; we never have to be hidden from his presence.

Thank you, Jesus, for staying with the plan and for bringing me back into your presence. Help me to live in a way that others will know you and come to salvation. Amen.

3. Slummin'

It is amazing that the King of Kings and Lord of Lords would come into this world that he created, and that he would come as a baby, born in a humble stable to working-class parents who had to flee for their lives from an evil ruler! It is even more astonishing that this king, knowing who he was in the hierarchy of the universe, would walk with common people, speaking to them and teaching them in terms that they would understand—seeds, fish, lamps, coins, pearls, and birds! This king used simple stories to explain himself to people who could never truly understand. He must have seen some beauty, some worth, and some potential in this world and in the lives he formed—even the ones who abandoned him—because he looked through loving eyes and left his perfect home to seek a bride.

Slummin' (or slumming) is a term that has been used for voluntarily visiting, interacting, and participating in the lives of people below one's social or economic level. It is, in effect, what Jesus did when he left heaven to step into time and become a man of this earth. He came down to our level and explained himself in a way so simple that farmers and fishermen, housewives and tax collectors, physicians, teachers, and even children could understand. He did not speak in the lofty language of heaven but in the common words of the daily lives of any who would hear. And to those who responded, and to those who respond still, he gave truth and eternal life with him in his perfect home.

Life indeed becomes a Cinderella story for those who receive

Jesus as Lord and King. For those who accept his proposal, he stoops down to make you great (2 Samuel 22:36).

Thank You, Jesus, for knowing everything about me—and loving me anyway! Amen.

4. Miracles

Jesus went to great lengths to prove to the people that he was who he said he was. He performed miracle after miracle, while inside he grieved over souls who were lost and bound for hell and only wanted to see a magic trick. Even Herod expected a performance when Jesus was sent to him: "And when Herod saw Jesus, he was greatly pleased, because for a long time he had been wanting to see him. From what he had heard about him, he hoped to see him perform some miracle" (Luke 23:8).

The day after Jesus had fed the five thousand (a very public demonstration of his great power and concern for his followers), and the day after he had walked on water (a more private reinforcement of his deity for the disciples), a group of fans sought out Jesus. Unbelievably, after what they had witnessed, the people asked Jesus, "What miraculous sign then will you give that we may see it and believe you? What will you do? Our forefathers ate manna in the desert; as it is written: He gave them bread from heaven to eat" (John 6:30–31). In other words, "You gave us one meal out of a loaf and a few fishes, but Moses fed a whole nation for forty years with manna from heaven. Give us something else to make us believe." And there is not a record of the disciples interrupting here to say, "Well, guess what we saw last night!" How frustrating!

This is the real miracle to me—that Jesus stayed calm and addressed the crowd with love and patience as he always did, as he always *does*. Are we so different from that crowd of fans? We still expect Jesus to reach into his "bag of tricks" at our demand. Many Christians today would rather base their faith on public spectacles and tingly feelings than on the promises of Christ. They would rather live on spiritual candy than on the Bread of Life. In spite of that, miraculously, Jesus is still reaching out, still interceding before the throne of grace, and still sending miracles. "For my Father's will is that everyone who looks to the Son and believes in him shall have eternal life, and I will raise him up at the last day" (John 6:40).

In addition, Jesus is still accepting our "loaves and fishes" in whatever way we offer them. In his hands, our small offerings can feed the hungry, our small acts of kindness can change stony hearts, our small prayers can heal big diseases. But the biggest miracle of all is this: Jesus knows everything about me, and about you, and he loves us anyway.

Lord, thank you that you still send miracles, and that sometimes you let us participate. Amen.

5. Mary and Martha

"Everyone should be quick to listen, slow to speak, and slow to become angry" (James 1:19). That all seems pretty cut and dry. With pride at the root of sin, one can understand why the Holy Spirit through James would write, "Be quick to listen" (for pride values its own way above others), "be slow to speak" (for pride values its own opinion over others), "be slow to become angry" (for pride values its own feelings over others). We know very well that, according to scripture, God is slow to anger and of great kindness (Numbers 14:18, Nehemiah 9:17, Psalm 86:15, Psalm 103:8, among others), and we also know that 1 Corinthians 13, in its definition of love, says that love is "slow to anger." Obviously, James gives us good and well-accepted advice about what it takes to get along with others. However, the more I meditated on this verse, the more I pictured Mary and Martha.

"As Jesus and his disciples were on their way, he came to a village where a woman named Martha opened up her home to him. She had a sister called Mary, who sat at the Lord's feet listening to what he said. But Martha was distracted by all the preparations that had to be made. She came to him and asked, 'Lord, don't you care that my sister has left me to do all the work by myself? Tell her to help me!'" (Luke 10:38–40).

Martha was flustered, but not for a bad reason or from a bad motive. Hospitality is a spiritual gift, right? And what a chance to show hospitality! Jesus and his followers were her guests! That in itself would be enough to cause me stress. I'm sure I would be like Martha, quite concerned about the food, its preparation and its presentation. It was because of her doubt about her ability to accomplish her task well, and possibly her fear of disappointing the Master, that Martha made a choice not to ask Mary why she chose to sit at the feet of Jesus instead of helping, but to get angry and complain to Jesus about her sister's behavior. The response was not what she wanted to hear. "Martha, Martha, you are worked up about things that will soon pass away; be quick to listen, slow to speak, and slow to become angry, for I would love for you to sit and hear my words like Mary is doing. The one who turned water into wine and fed the five thousand is not stressed about the preparation of the meal." Well, that is my extended scene.

When I have on my "hospitality cap," it is difficult for me not to stress about the condition of my home or the quality of my meals, especially as an Italian Grammy. I mean, food and hospitality are what we do! But God is working on me, too. More and more often, I find myself at the feet of Jesus first and foremost—before I cook, before I clean, before I make my lesson plans or grade papers. It means I don't have as much time for other things, but in the end I don't want to hear, "Beverly, Beverly, you are anxious and troubled about many things." I want to hear, "Well done, good and faithful servant," and the only way to accomplish that is to get as close to Jesus as I possibly can.

Lord Jesus, instill in my heart the desires of Mary, and free me from the stresses of Martha, inasmuch as it will serve your plans for my life today and every day. Amen.

How's the Family?

6. Part of the Family

I grew up in a small town on the Ohio River where, in times gone by, immigrants poured into the area to work in the coal mines and steel mills that lined its banks. There was a large Italian community there, and folks seemed to recognize when one belonged to that community even before they knew a last name. People in that group were blue collar, Catholic, for the most part, had similar physical characteristics, gathered in extended family groups for holidays, and even had similar speech patterns. I was one of them, but when I got older and moved away from home, I was not often recognized as part of that group, especially since the Italian name is on my mother's side. However, I was sure that no matter where I went, and no matter how long I was gone, when I returned, the family would know me and receive me again.

There is another family in which I grew up. In 1 John 3:9–10 we read, "No one who is born of God will continue to sin, because God's seed (Gk: *sperma*) remains in him; he cannot go on sinning, because he has been born of God. This is how we know who the children of God are and who the children of the devil are: Anyone who does not do what is right is not a child of God; nor is anyone who does not love his brother." Just as there were certain characteristics that came through my Italian bloodline, there are certain characteristics that come through the bloodline of Christ. Just as the world did not always recognize God in Christ, it does not always recognize his progeny, particularly if we choose to wander out into the world. "The light shines in the darkness and the darkness has not understood it. He was in the world, and though the world was made through him, the world did not recognize him. He came to that which was his own, but his own did not receive him. Yet to all those who received him, to those who believed on his name, he gave the right to become the children of God—children not born of natural descent, nor of human decision or a husband's will, but born of God" (John 1:5, 10–13); "How great is the love the Father has lavished on us, that we should be called children of God! And that is what we are! The reason the world does not know us is that it did not know him" (1 John 3:1).

I knew a Kindergarten teacher once who continually poured her whole energy into her classroom. She invested hours of her off time, abundant energy, and probably thousands of dollars into her classroom. People asked her all the time, "Why are you doing all this? They don't pay you enough for this!" Her response was just to smile and say, "Well, the children enjoy it." Other people did not understand why she did the things she did. I knew her well, and I knew that she did it because she genuinely cared about her students and their welfare and education, and that the school could not afford to offer her compensation. For some odd reason, many of the other teachers in the school resented her. Did I say she was a Christian, a part of the "family of God"? The world does not always understand why we do what we do, and often people resent what they do not understand; at best, they don't trust in what they do not understand. Nothing in life is free, right?

There is a community, a *family*, in which we will always be known, loved and accepted in spite of our mistakes and imperfections or the opinions of others. In that family, there is a commonality of purpose, goals, work, speech, and most of all, love. We have the choice to receive and to be received by that family. It is hard to stand alone, but God has given us brothers and sisters to lift us up, and he has made us heirs and joint-heirs of his kingdom.

Abba, Father, thank you for your family, our family, the family of God! Amen.

7. Family Likeness

A few times I was blessed to be able to go on vacation with my extended family, four generations of us. It is always amusing to me, although it happens far too seldom, to go somewhere with my mother, my daughter and my grand-daughters, and to ultimately have someone recognize the relationship and comment about how much we look (and even act) alike. As much as I enjoy that, the one I really want to be told that I resemble is my Daddy. You know him—Daddy with the capital *D*, our Abba, Father.

This family likeness means more than just being called by the Father's name, or even being seen with him. It literally means taking on his characteristics. The more time we spend with someone, the more we tend to act or react in the same way as that someone, and most of the time it is not done consciously. I know that to look like him, I need to put off my old likeness and put on the "new self, created to be like God in true righteousness and holiness" (Ephesians 4:24).

We are exhorted, "Therefore, as God's chosen people, holy and dearly loved, clothe yourselves with compassion, kindness, humility, gentleness, and patience. Bear with each other and forgive whatever grievances you may have against one another. Forgive as the Lord forgave you. And over all these virtues, put on love, which binds them all together in perfect unity. Let the peace of Christ rule in your hearts, since as members of one body you were called in peace. And be thankful. Let the word of Christ dwell in you richly as you teach and admonish one another with all wisdom, and as you sing psalms, hymns and spiritual songs, with gratitude in your hearts to God. And whatever you do, whether in word or deed, do it all in the name of the Lord Jesus, giving thanks to God the Father through him" (Colossians 3:12–17).

There are a lot of action verbs in there, a lot of *works*, and although I realize that I am not saved by works, because I love my Daddy, I do my best. Sometimes the works seem difficult, but I try, and with his help, I'm getting better. I want to hear people say, "You look just like your Daddy." I want to be recognized because of his family likeness.

Lord, you are the potter and I am the clay. Help me to look like you! Amen

8. Inheritance

When I think of the word *inheritance*, I get mixed images. I suppose most of the time people think of money, antiques, property or jewelry as an inheritance, and in some ways I do, too, but there are other facets of my life that I also consider an inheritance.

I inherited a love of books from my mother. Many of my most vivid memories of her from my childhood involve books. She was always reading, so she set the example, and she made sure there were books in the house that were appropriate and engaging for my brother and me. I inherited from her the idea that one should be in church on Sunday mornings and that one should trust God and pray. I don't remember hearing her pray out loud often, but I knew she prayed. I knew she prayed for me. My mother also passed on the idea of being strong in difficult situations and rolling with the punches. She raised my brother and me as a single parent and helped to provide for her own widowed mother, so she was well acquainted with sacrifice. The word *can't* was not a part of her vocabulary, and she didn't expect to hear it from us. I remember her telling my daughter once, "Always remember that you are a strong woman and you come from a line of strong women." She didn't talk about these concepts much; she modeled them always.

From her mother, my grandmother, I inherited a love of cooking and baking. The quintessential Italian grandma, she was often to be found in her spotless kitchen making wonderful things to eat—bread and pasta from scratch, cookies, sugar-cinnamon "twisties," meatballs with sauce … I get hungry just thinking about it. I didn't get to help often, but when I did, especially as the Christmas holidays approached, she ingrained in me the right way to do things in the kitchen—use good ingredients and don't skimp. "Use enough, but not too much." The more she baked, the more she gave away. Grandma didn't have much, truly not much in the eyes of the world, but she knew how to give. She taught me giving.

From my Grammy and Grampy, I inherited creativity. My Grampy was a lapidary, and he was often at his workbench in the basement of his house making beautiful things: pendants, earrings, rings, and tie pins made of jade, onyx, agate, and various other semi-precious stones. He taught me how to do it when I was pretty young, and I loved spending time with him in his workshop. As a side lesson, he taught me the value of quietness. We never talked much in those hours I spent with him (he whistled more than he talked), but I could feel the closeness we shared.

On the other hand, Grammy talked all the time. She was also very artsy and taught me how to color eggs with beeswax and dye, how to etch flowers and birds on silver platters, how to make flowers out of fake fur, how to make wreaths out of pine cones and twigs, and how to manipulate beads, pom-poms, fabric, wire and glue. She even helped me to turn some of that into a profitable enterprise to make my own money for Christmas. In my twenties, I loved going to the ceramic shop with her when I could. One of my prized possessions is the Nativity set she made in the ceramic shop, and that I inherited when she passed away and Grampy sold their house.

They always taught me things that I never realized I was learning. They showed me bird nests with baby birds, how tulips can be planted in various colors and come back the next year in one composite color (and the part the bees play in that magic), how to change the color of Queen Anne's Lace, what happens to a grasshopper when it gets too close to a praying mantis, how to "skin the cat" on the playground monkey bars, how to invent a tool if you don't have one that will work, how to give and not let people know you're doing it, and how to be a friend. They also taught me that life is fun, and that you can joke and laugh when you're a Christian, and God's good with that.

From my dad (who came into my life when I was twenty), I inherited a sense of responsibility and support. I was not often at home after he and my mother married, but I felt so much better about living far away because I knew that no matter what happened, he was going to take care of things. He was there for his mother, he was there for my grandmother, he has always been there for my mother, and no matter how many times this prodigal daughter returned home, he never turned me away.

None of those people were extremely wealthy, but they left me a rich inheritance. Like Peter who said, "Silver and gold I do not have, but what I have, I give you" (Acts 3:6), my family gave me, and continues to give me, so much that is beyond the value of silver and gold.

There is a futile inheritance, the one based on money, antiques, property, jewelry, and the like, that can be lost, stolen, or pilfered away. There can also be an inheritance of worry, fear, selfishness, anger, discontent, and other intangibles that we can pass on to our children, even if we are unaware that we are doing it. We must be careful what we model.

Jesus said, "Do not store up for yourselves treasures on earth, where moth and rust destroy and where thieves break in and steal. But store up for yourselves treasures in heaven, where moth and rust do not destroy and where thieves do not break in and steal. For where your treasure is, there your heart will be also" (Matthew 6:19–21). I am blessed every day by my eternal inheritance through Jesus Christ my Lord. I am grateful every day for the family in which God placed me, and for the indestructible inheritance I was given.

Lord, I pray that I may leave a valuable inheritance for my family. Amen.

9. The Big Water

Several years ago we took a trip to Savannah, Georgia. I was blessed to accompany my granddaughters on their first trip to the beach. Although one of the girls was just a couple weeks old, the other was nearly two, and able to talk about it. We conversed for days about going to the "big water." We discussed seeing the waves and how they would feel and taste. I even bought her some sand toys to play with on the beach.

When the moment finally came and we stepped along the boardwalk over the dunes, I told her, "In just a second we're going to see the 'big water'!" Excited, but unable to keep the pace with her little legs, she said, "Hold you me," and reached up her little arms for me to carry her, and, of course, I did! Then we topped the dune and the glorious, sunny panorama of the whole eastern Atlantic opened up before us! I set her down expecting awe and exclamations. Instead, she went for her bucket and shovel! She didn't even perceive the "big water," only the sand that she could grab with her tiny hands and her toys. She was also fascinated by sticks and shells and pieces of seaweed that she found. She had a blast!

I contemplated that for a long time that day, and finally came to the conclusion that the "big water" was just too much for her twenty-month-old mind to comprehend. The sand was something with which she was relatively familiar from the sandbox at daycare. She knew what to do with it; she could hold it, she could understand it. It wasn't until later that afternoon when she saw her mother and me walking to the edge and getting our feet wet and splashing a little in the waves that she became interested at all in trying that out. When she did, she loved it, and before the afternoon was over, we had a real little beach bunny.

We can be like that with God. He really is way too big for our mortal minds to understand—a being who operates out of space and time, the one who created everything out of nothing, the God who is bigger and mightier than the deepest ocean or the highest mountain—so we turn to that with which we are familiar, the things we can understand and manipulate.

After my grandmother's funeral, I asked my brother, one of the smartest people I've ever known, what he thought about life after death. He looked thoughtful for a moment, then said something I will never forget. He said it's like imagining God as a basketball and the world as a piece of paper. The basketball can roll all over that paper, but at no time can the paper experience, understand or receive the whole ball, because the ball has dimensions that the paper does not have. Even if the ball were to somehow pass through the paper, the paper could only receive part of the ball at a time. There is so much more to it than we are able to understand and receive in our flesh.

When we seek explanations and predictions about God that fit our human logic, more often than not, we will be unsatisfied. "As the heavens are higher than the earth, so are my ways higher than your ways and my thoughts than your thoughts" (Isaiah 55:9). Leaving ego behind, we realize that God is God, and there are some things we are just not going to understand fully. However, the glorious, sunny panorama of eternity is waiting for those who are willing to look beyond what they can control and manipulate and understand, and we are invited to come in faith and splash in the waves.

Lord God, thank you for all your creation—the things we can understand, and the things we can't. Amen.

10. Seek His Face

"Come to me all you who are burdened," "Come near to God and he will come near to you," "If you seek the Lord your God you will find him, if you look for him with all your heart and with all your soul." Truly the scriptures tell us that the Lord our God desires a relationship with his people, his sons and daughters, with *us*. I reflect on the New Testament relationships of Jesus with those who drew close to him: Mary, who sat at his feet; John, who reclined against him at the table; Peter, who walked to him on the water; the woman who poured perfume on his feet and wiped them with her hair; the children who were drawn to him. So many who lived with Jesus had the opportunity for physical contact with him. It is one of the saddest revelations I have ever come upon that the only mention of anyone literally seeking his *face* was Judas who kissed him to betray him.

Still, Jesus has not hidden his face from us. Still, he calls us to come. Still, he loves and desires us. Unbelievable! Unfathomable! *Unnatural!* I love Psalm 27:8: "My heart says of you, 'Seek his face!' Your face, Lord, I will seek."

I remember when my children were small and they needed my attention. They didn't bow at my feet or recline against me. Feet and laps were OK for things like watching movies or playing games, but when they were hurt or frightened or exhausted, they put their little cheeks against my cheek and their little arms around my neck. And when they wanted a kiss, they went for the face. They weren't willing to put it off until after a "ceremonial cleansing" either. When they needed something, they got up close, looked me

22

in the eye, and . . . contact! In short, for the important stuff, they sought my *face*.

Our awesome, Abba Daddy has invited us to do the same thing with him—to be his children as he created us to be. I'm honored for the times when I can kneel before his majesty, and I am humbled by the times when I can worship at his feet, but I am saved by the times when I can reach for his beautiful face, the times when I can come to him as his child in full assurance of his unconditional love and grace.

Your face, Lord, do I seek. Amen

11. As a Child

One of the great things about children is that they *believe* and *believe in* their grown-ups.

I am told that my first grade teacher got a real laugh out of my announcement that "My grandfather can do anything!" It was all the more amusing because she actually graduated from high school with him. Yes, if Grampy said it, I believed it! When I was pretty young, I noticed his toothbrush in the medicine cabinet. It had the brush on one end of the handle and one of those rubber picks on the other end. I was curious about it and asked him one day what that "rubber thing" on his toothbrush was. He answered, "That's what I use to clean between my toes." I was disgusted, but I believed him. In fact, I believed it until I was in high school! As the years went by, I learned to recognize his sense of humor, but my belief in him never changed much. He's still one of the greatest men I've ever known.

A long time ago, I had a refrigerator that made some pretty crazy noises. It would gurgle and growl and pop, not just once in a while, but all the time. One day my four-year-old son asked me, a little fearfully, "Mama, what's that noise?" Being the kind and sensitive parent I was, I answered, "That's the food trying to get out." My poor son wouldn't go back into the kitchen for days! I guess I am, in many ways, like my grandfather.

Jesus seemed to find joy in the company of children. "The disciples came to Jesus and asked, 'Who is the greatest in the kingdom of heaven?' He called a little child and had him stand among them. And he said: 'I tell you the truth, unless you change and become like little children, you will never enter the kingdom of heaven. Therefore, whoever humbles himself like this child is the greatest in the kingdom of heaven'" (Matthew 18:1–2). "People were bringing little children to Jesus to have him touch them, but the disciples rebuked them. When Jesus saw this, he was indignant. He said to them, 'Let the little children come to me, and do not hinder them, for the kingdom of God belongs to such as these. I tell you the truth, anyone who will not receive the kingdom of God like a little child will never enter it.' And he took the children in his arms, put his hands on them, and blessed them" (Mark 10:13–16).

Children believe their grown-ups. Jesus could have revealed any of the deep secrets of heaven to those children, and they would have believed and had no doubt, just because of who he was. Unfortunately, in this age in which we live, many are taught very young not to trust and not to believe in the things that cannot be perceived with the five physical senses or understood based on logic and academics—the things that aren't *real*. But even Shakespeare said, "There are more things in heaven and earth than are dreamt of in your philosophy." Jesus prayed, "I praise you, Father, Lord of heaven and earth, for you have hidden these things from the wise and learned, and revealed them to little children. Yes, Father, for this was your good pleasure" (Matthew 11:25–26).

Does that mean we are not allowed to ask questions? Of course not! Children are masters of the art of asking questions. "Why?" "Are we there yet?" "When are we gonna be there?" "Why?" "Is supper ready yet?" "When is it gonna be ready?" "Why?" Do I have to?" "Why?"

The Lord says, "Call to me and I will answer you and tell you great and unsearchable things you do not know" (Jeremiah 33:3); "But when he, the Spirit of Truth, comes, he will guide you into all truth. He will not speak on his own; he will speak only what he hears, and he will tell you what is yet to come" (John 16:13). The secret to getting answers from God is to *listen*. Remember Elijah, who sought a word from God: "Then a great and powerful wind tore the mountains apart and shattered rocks before the Lord, but the Lord was not in the wind. After the wind there was an earthquake, but the Lord was not in the earthquake. After the earthquake came a fire, but the Lord was not in the fire. And after the fire came a gentle whisper," and in the whisper, Elijah found his answer! (1Kings 19:11–12). He asked for God, and then he hung in there like a rusty fishhook until God showed up. He waited with the stubborn will of a child!

My mother used to refer to me as Peter Pan because I never wanted to grow up. Now that I am older, I still prefer to remain as much a child as is possible in my adult world, and as a child, I ask, I believe, and I receive what my Lord says, just because he says it. Oh, I ask questions sometimes, and once in a while I throw a tantrum, but he understands, and he loves me anyway because I'm his child.

Lord, please help me to remain a child in all the important ways. Amen.

The Family Business: Tending the Flock

12. Sheep's Clothing

Sheep have a reputation for being, well, unintelligent. They are very social animals who stick close together and congregate. Their greatest threat is from predators and parasites. When they perceive danger, their best defense is to run, but when cornered, they stamp and charge, for all the good it does. Although not the smartest of animals, sheep can learn to recognize a human when exposed to that human over a period of time, to recognize the emotions demonstrated on his face, and even to trust that individual to lead them to still water to drink and safe food to eat.

I wear sheep's clothing. There were numerous occasions in my life when I made very unintelligent decisions and reactions. I prefer to be around people I know well, those I recognize and trust. When I perceive danger, I usually try to get out of Dodge. I'm not confrontational. When pushed, I may make a show of ferocity, but I'm not very convincing. I know that my worst enemy is "prowling around like a roaring lion seeking for someone to devour." Sometimes his attacks come from the outside in the form of lack, sickness, or trouble on the job. Sometimes they come from the inside in the form of worry, grief, anger, envy or wrong thinking.

But I have this shepherd. I know his voice and he calls me by my name, and I come. I trust my shepherd to have my best interest at heart. He is always merciful, he is always kind, and I always know that he loves me. He feeds my mind, body and spirit with good things. He protects me from harm, and though I am sometimes confronted by the wickedness of this world, sometimes preyed upon by evil, he is ready with a rod in his capable hands to defend me. He died to save me, his sheep. And although to the world, this may all seem unintelligent, I will stay as close to him as I can.

I may not be a born leader, nor am I much of a warrior, but I am a very good sheep, and sometimes I wear steel wool.

Dear Jesus, I will stay close to you and trust you always. Amen

13. My Shepherd

Several years ago, my ninety-four-year-old grandmother lay in the hospital. She had a number of things wrong with her body and had been living in a nursing home for a couple of years where she could get the care she so desperately needed. My mom and dad lived close enough that they could visit her every day. If I can't say Grandma did really well, I can at least say she maintained her spark for many months; however, she eventually declined and had to be taken to the hospital.

While in the hospital, my grandmother became unresponsive. One day the doctor approached my mother during a visit to inform her that my grandmother's kidneys were failing. Mom asked about what could be done and was told they could start dialysis, but that it would be very uncomfortable for Grandma. Mom asked the doctor what she would recommend, and the doctor offered the options, none of which provided much comfort or hope. "I just wish I could have a sign what to do," my mom responded. Understand that my grandmother had not conversed or even reacted to company for a while, but when my mother went back to her, my grandmother said clearly, "The Lord is my shepherd, and I'm not sad about this." My mother had her sign, and without further conversation, my grandmother passed into the arms of her shepherd very soon afterward.

Jesus said, "The man who enters by the gate is the shepherd of his sheep. The watchman opens the gate for him, and the sheep listen to his voice. He calls his own sheep by name and leads them out. When he has brought out all his own, he goes on ahead of

them, and his sheep follow him, because they know his voice"
(John 10:2–4).

Sickness and the deterioration of old age attempted to overcome
my grandmother, but in the end, they could only overcome her
flesh because her spirit was confidently following her Lord. "The
thief comes only to steal and kill and destroy. I have come that they
may have life, and have it to the full. I am the good shepherd. The
good shepherd lays down his life for the sheep" (John 10:10–11).
Because Jesus won the victory over death, hell and the grave, my
grandmother is also victorious. I know that today she is healthy and
happy and alive with her Good Shepherd, and someday I'm going
to join them, because he's my shepherd, too.

Lead me, my Good Shepherd. I will follow you. Amen.

14. With Haste

I want to talk about another group of shepherds. The Gospel of Luke, Chapter Two, tells that on the night that our Good Shepherd was born as a baby into this world, "there were in the same country, shepherds abiding in the field, keeping watch over their flock by night. And, lo, the angel of the Lord came upon them, and the glory of the Lord shone round about them, and they were sore afraid. And the angel said unto them, Fear not: for, behold, I bring you good tidings of great joy, which shall be to all people. For unto you is born this day in the city of David, a Saviour, which is Christ the Lord. And this shall be a sign unto you; you shall find the babe wrapped in swaddling clothes, lying in a manger. And suddenly there was with the angel a multitude of the heavenly host praising God and saying, Glory to God in the highest, and on earth peace, good will toward men" (8–14 KJV).

There they were, these shepherds, at work on a seemingly ordinary night. Their job: tending to those poor, unintelligent, vulnerable sheep. They were not looking for a sign in the heavens; they were watching for predators. They were not noble in the eyes of the world; they were humble, low, and dirty. They were not waiting for an announcement, but when the announcement came, they were afraid! And afterward, their response: "Let us go even unto Bethlehem, and see this thing which is come to pass, which the Lord hath made known unto us. And so they came *with haste*" (15).

The shepherds at work on the hills of Bethlehem were a rugged lot. I say "at work" because that is exactly what it was. Sometimes the owner of the sheep or family members cared for the flocks, but most often it was hired men who lived day and night with the sheep, walking long distances and keeping track of every last lamb, making sure they had fields in which to graze and still water from which to drink. It was a job for *responsible* employees, not men or women who would walk off in the middle of the night on a whim. Yet, these shepherds went, and went without permission or preparation. They believed the angel and wanted to be a part of the miracle of the long-foretold nativity of the Messiah. The angel did not say the salvation of these shepherds depended upon their decision to go to the stable. There may have been some who chose not to go. But those who went became a part of one of the greatest miracles of all time, the coming of God into human flesh, the beginning of the fulfillment of the promise made in Genesis 3.

I wonder how many times God has spoken to people to announce a coming miracle. I wonder how many people have not heard the voice of the angel for the noise in their lives. I wonder how many people have heard the announcement, but have dismissed it as imagination, or how many have heard it and did not feel they could go because they had other responsibilities. Miracles happen all the time, and God calls for witnesses now as he did then. Have you heard a call to go and pray for someone, or to go to an evangelist's meeting, or to go on a mission trip, and been too busy or afraid to respond? If your answer to that question is yes, I would bet that you are in the majority. Most of us try to be reliable and responsible to the obligations of this world, and believe me, I'm not trying to condemn reliability, but how many miracles do we miss out on because we dismiss the announcement of the angels, or the whisper of God? My prayer is that the next time I hear the call, wherever I am and whatever I am doing, I will go *with haste*, not because my salvation depends on it, but because to be in the center of what God is doing is always the very best place to be.

Heavenly Father, help me to listen with my spiritual ears, and when you call, give me the faith to go with haste! Amen.

15. The Lamb of God

Jesus Christ, the Good Shepherd, was also paradoxically the sacrificial Lamb "slain from the foundation of the world." He was revealed as such long before he came to earth in the flesh. When John recognized Jesus as he approached on the river bank, he did not say, "Behold the Messiah," or "Behold the one who has come to save us," but "Behold the Lamb."

Perhaps the first instance of the sacrifice of an animal on behalf of sinful humans was way back in the Garden of Eden. When Adam and Eve recognized the meaning of their nakedness, "the Lord made garments of skin for Adam and his wife and clothed them" (Genesis 3:21 NIV). The Bible doesn't say what kind of animal had to die to create the garments that covered the nakedness of Adam and Eve, but I have heard the suggestion that it was a lamb.

On another occasion, Abraham was instructed to sacrifice his son on an altar. Isaac questioned his father Abraham, "The fire and wood are here, but where is the lamb for the burnt offering?" Abraham prophetically answered, "God himself will provide the lamb." In Abraham, God found a man of his creation who was willing to sacrifice his beloved son out of faith, obedience and trust, opening up the door for God to offer the same sacrifice of his beloved Son. God intervened on behalf of Abraham's son, indeed, sending a substitute for Isaac, a ram caught in the bushes. Then, when the time was right, God sent his own beloved Son Jesus Christ as a sacrifice for us, the sons and daughters of sinful humanity, who deserve death. "Was not our ancestor Abraham considered righteous for what he did when he offered his son Isaac on the altar? You see that his faith and his actions were working together and his faith was made complete by what he did. And the scripture was fulfilled that says, 'Abraham believed God, and it was credited to him as righteousness,' and he was called God's friend" (James 2:21–23). In Abraham's case, God sent a lamb; In God's case, Jesus Christ was the Lamb.

In Exodus 12, we read how the Lord spoke to Moses and Aaron saying, "Tell the whole community of Israel that on the tenth day of this month, each man is to take a lamb for his family, one for each household. If any household is too small for a whole lamb, they must share one with their nearest neighbor … The animals you choose must be year-old males without defect, and you may take them from the sheep or the goats. Take care of them until the fourteenth day of the month, when all the people of the community of Israel must slaughter them at twilight. Then they are to take some of the blood and put it on the sides and tops of the door-frames of the houses where they eat the lambs … Do not eat the meat raw or cooked in water, but roast it over the fire—head, legs and inner parts. Do not leave any of it till morning … The blood will be a sign for you on the houses where you are; and when I see the blood, I will pass over you. No destructive plague will touch you when I strike Egypt" (Exodus 12:3–12). The people were instructed to use the *whole lamb,* not just their favorite parts or the parts they might choose, just the same as we must accept *all of Christ,* not just the parts we pick and choose. When we live in Christ, the spotless Lamb, his blood is a sign over us, and we receive salvation through him.

Lambs and goats continued to be sacrificed for the burnt offerings as a demonstration of commitment and devotion to God and as atonement for unintentional sin (Leviticus 1, 6:8–13, 8:18–21), as an act of worship for the fellowship offering (3, 7:11–34), as atonement for sins and cleansing from defilement (4:1–5, 13, 6:24–38, 8:14–17, 16:3–22), and as restitution and cleansing for the guilt offering (5:14–6:7, 7:1–6). Particularly fascinating is the direction for the *scapegoat.* "Then [Aaron] is to take the two goats and present them before the Lord at the entrance to the Tent of Meeting. He is to cast lots for the two goats—one lot for the Lord and the other for the scapegoat. Aaron shall bring the goat whose lot falls to the Lord and sacrifice it for a sin offering. But the goat chosen by lot as the scapegoat shall be presented alive before the Lord to be used for making atonement by sending it into the desert as a scapegoat ... When Aaron has finished making atonement for the Most Holy Place, the Tent of Meeting and the altar, he shall bring forward the live goat. He is to lay both hands on the head of the live goat and confess over it all the wickedness and rebellion of the Israelites—all their sins—and put them on the goat's head. He shall send the goat away into the desert in the care of a man appointed for the task. The goat will carry on itself all their sins to a solitary place; and the man shall release it into the desert" (16:7–10, 20–22). Jesus was our scapegoat. As he went out into that desert place alone on Calvary, he carried our sins far away, and on the cross, they died with him under the flow of his precious blood.

Did John see all this when Jesus walked up to him on the bank of the Jordan? How completely he understood the symbolism of his statement, we cannot know. But in these days as the scripture has been revealed, we do recognize Jesus Christ as the one who covered our guilt, the one who caused death to pass us by, and the one who carried our sins away upon himself. Hebrews 9:2b reminds us that "without the shedding of blood, there is no forgiveness," and a few verses later comforts us with the words, "So Christ was sacrificed once to take away the sins of many people; and he will appear a second time, not to bear sin, but to bring salvation to those who are waiting for him" (9:28).

Lord Jesus, thank you for your sacrifice. Help me never, never to take it for granted. Amen.

A Walk
in the
Garden

16. Seeds, Roots, and Trees

Back in the days when I taught kindergarten, I taught the children a song about plants. It was sung to the tune of "Frere Jacques," and the words went like this:

Plants need water (plants need water)
Light and soil (light and soil)
So they'll grow (so they'll grow)
So they'll grow (so they'll grow)

The poetry leaves a lot to be desired, but the kids got the message—there are certain things that seeds absolutely cannot do without if they are to become grown, healthy, and productive plants. This is a microcosm of the kingdom of God. It is amazing to me how God teaches us the great lessons of the kingdom as we observe the little things in the world he made!

As in the song, people need spiritual water, light and soil to become what God has ordained for them to be.

There are several symbols in the Bible to represent the Holy Spirit and one of those symbols is water. "Whoever believes in me, as the Scripture has said, streams of living water will flow from within him" (John 7:38); "Whoever drinks the water I give him will never thirst. Indeed, the water I give him will become in him a spring of water welling up to eternal life" (John 4:14); "For we were all baptized by one Spirit into one body … and we were all given one Spirit to drink" (1 Cor. 12:13); "This is he who came by water [spirit] and blood [humanity]—Jesus Christ. He did not come by water only, but by water and blood. And it is the Spirit who testifies, because the Spirit is truth" (1 John 5:6).

Have you ever opened up a dry butterbean? Inside there is a tiny plant shape—but it is still only a *potential* plant. If you soak that butterbean in water, very shortly the tiny plant will emerge from its shell. That butterbean is like people. We all contain potential gifts that God has placed within us. Those gifts emerge when we soak ourselves in the Holy Spirit.

A plant also needs a source of light—the sun (or, we might cleverly say, the Son). The first chapter of the gospel of John says in verses 1–4, "In the beginning was the Word, and the Word was with God, and the Word was God. He was with God in the beginning. Through him all things were made; without him nothing was made that has been made. In him was life, and that life was the *light* of men." Jesus himself claimed, "I am the *light* of the world" (John 8:12 and 9:5). Just as plants need sunlight to produce chlorophyll for their sustenance, we need Jesus Christ, the light who becomes the bread of life. He instigates the production of the spiritual food necessary for our eternal life.

Then comes the soil. The baby plants need a place to sprout roots and become mature. You know where we're going, Matthew 13—the parable of the sower and the seed. Jesus taught that the seed, or the Word, is scattered, and some falls on rocky places, some among thorns, some onto shallow soil, and some onto good, fertile soil. Of course, bad things happen to the seed that goes anywhere but the good, fertile soil. The soil is the *heart* of a person. The literal translation of the word *heart,* either in the Old Testament (Pharaoh's *heart* was hardened) or the New Testament ("It was because your *hearts* were hard") is the thoughts and feelings. A farmer prepares the ground for planting by breaking up the clumps of dirt and removing the stones. God says he will remove a heart of stone and give us a heart of flesh. So we pray with David, "Create in me a pure heart, O God, and renew a steadfast spirit within me" (Psalm 51:10). Break up my clumps and remove my hard-heartedness; make me ready for your seed. The nutrients rise from the soil through the roots and travel to the outermost branches and leaves of a tree. If the soil is bad or inadequate, the tree will not produce good fruit.

So, say we have a healthy tree growing in good soil, and know that we have the promise of good fruit, but we're not seeing much. I remember when I was pretty young, I liked to plant flowers in my backyard. Unfortunately, I was not very patient. I planted my seeds, watered them, and observed the sun hitting the soil where the seeds had been sown for some extended long period (like two days), and if I could see nothing happening, I began to dig around a little with my fingers, just to make sure something *was* happening. What I usually found was that tiny roots had begun to work their way down out of the seeds and deeper into the rich earth. Even though I couldn't see it, growth was taking place just as it should. The flowers would have been in trouble if long stems and heavy buds had come up before they had something to secure and anchor them to their life-giving soil! Ecclesiastes 3 tells us that "There is a time for everything, and a season for every activity under heaven," and God himself has ordained those times and seasons in the life of a plant, and in the life of a human being. And just like the tree can't decide on its own when it is time to bud, flower, or produce fruit, but has to wait for the ordained time, you and I can't decide when and how our own fruit should arrive, and particularly not when and how we should see the fruit of someone else. Remember those plants I dug around to see if anything was happening? Sometimes my digging caused a delay in a plant's development, and sometimes it caused its death. Too much tampering can hinder what God is doing.

God is always at work in his children, and whether we see it or not, "he who began a good work in you will carry it on to completion" (Philippians 1:6). By the way, patience is a *fruit* of the spirit! God has all things under control and we can trust him.

I want to be like the tree in Psalm 1: "Blessed is the man who does not walk in the counsel of the wicked or stand in the way of sinners or sit in the seat of mockers. But his delight is in the law of the Lord, and on his law he meditates day and night. He is like a tree planted by the streams of water, which yields its fruit in season and whose leaf does not wither. Whatever he does prospers."

Hosea instructs, "Sow for yourselves righteousness, reap the fruit of unfailing love, and break up your unplowed ground; for it is time to seek the Lord until he comes and showers righteousness on you" (10:12).

Lord of the harvest, help me to sow good seed and produce good fruit for your kingdom's sake. Amen.

17. Up on the Farm

I recently received an email from a former student. Part of it went like this:

"In December of last year I became a believer after having a couple of my sorority sisters invest in me and get me involved with campus outreach and pulling me to them instead of letting me get caught up in the stereotypical sorority college life. Really no one at home knows the life I was living or knows the stuff I was falling into, but it was crammed with rebellion and sin and disgusting stuff. I knew about God and who he was, what Christ did, and the whole gospel through and through, but I thought there was no way I was worth any of it. I remember you telling our class your testimony once, and it made a lasting impression in my heart and mind about his love. I tried to push it out, because it was just another thing reminding me of the sin I was living in, and I was fairly successful in doing so. Then this summer at a beach project which is a campus outreach program, we were working on developing our own testimonies and sharing them with other people, which was something I was very reluctant to do and I avoided it as long as I could. I remembered again the story you told us that day. I was overwhelmed all over again by God's love and I had a much bigger desire to share the story of how he changed my heart. Realizing that you opened up yourself and your heart and life to us even though probably very few of us actually got the message was just amazing to me."

That was the story of a seed. Please, realize that I brag on God alone, and not on myself. I'm just so grateful that he used me. There were several others who worked in the field in this seed's story—thank God for those sorority sisters! "What, after all, is Apollos? And what is Paul? Only servants, through whom you came to believe—as the Lord has assigned to each his task. I planted the seed, Apollos watered it, but God made it grow. So neither he who plants nor he who waters is anything, but only God, who makes things grow. The man who plants and the man who waters have one purpose, and each will be rewarded according to his own labor. For we are God's fellow workers; you are God's field, God's building" (1 Corinthians 3:5–9).

From time to time the Lord moves on my heart to do things. Once in a while it's to pray for someone; sometimes it's a word of knowledge or encouragement or prophecy; sometimes it's something a little strange. For example, many years ago the Lord prompted me to make business-sized cards for each member of the graduating class. On one side I was supposed to put a quotation that was familiar and meaningful to all of us, and on the other side I was supposed to pray and fast and seek an individual scripture for each student. Right before graduation every year since, I have presented these cards to the seniors, just asking that they put them in their wallets or billfolds, and telling them that my prayer is that on the day they need encouragement, direction, or a word from the Lord, they will find their card. A couple years ago, I considered giving it up. Making the cards takes a lot of time during my busiest time of year, and the materials were getting expensive. Besides, I never heard that anyone was benefitting from them. Then the testimonies started coming in—three ex-students within a short period of time told me how the card had spoken to them in a moment of need, or how the verse was just the thing they needed to share with a suffering friend. Of course, I have continued to make the cards. It's just sowing seeds that God has given to me.

We often consider our offerings of money to be our seeds. Although they can be, our seeds are not always money. God has given us other seeds and much equipment to work on his farm: "To one there is given through the Spirit the message of wisdom, to another the message of knowledge by means of the same Spirit, to another faith by the same Spirit, to another gifts of healing by that one Spirit, to another miraculous powers, to another prophesy, to another distinguishing between spirits, to another speaking in different kinds of tongues, and to still another the interpretation of tongues. All these are the work of one and the same Spirit, and he gives them to each one, just as he determines" (1 Corinthians 12:8–11); "In the church God has appointed first of all apostles, second prophets, third teachers, then workers of miracles, also those having gifts of healing, those able to help others, those with gifts of administration, and those speaking in different kinds of tongues" (28); "It was [Christ] who gave some to be apostles, some to be prophets, some to be evangelists, and some to be pastors and teachers, to prepare God's people for works of service, so that the body of Christ may be built up" (Ephesians 4:11–12). Our seed can be anything we plant for the body of Christ, from preaching in the pulpit, to watching the nursery, to cleaning the church restrooms, to being "the good Samaritan" (speaking of whom, notice how we are never given his name—often we sow our seed anonymously).

"Remember this: Whoever sows sparingly will also reap sparingly, and whoever sows generously will also reap generously. Each man should give what he has decided in his heart to give, not reluctantly or under compulsion, for God loves a cheerful giver. And God is able to make all grace abound to you, so that in all things at all times, having all that you need, you will abound in every good work. As it is written: 'He has scattered abroad his gifts to the poor; his righteousness endures forever.' Now he who supplies seed to the sower and bread for food will also supply and increase your store of seed and will enlarge the harvest of your righteousness. You will be made rich in every way so that you can be generous on every occasion, and through us your generosity will result in thanksgiving to God. This service that you perform is not only supplying the needs of God's people but is also overflowing in many expressions of thanks to God. Because of the service by which you have proved yourselves, men will praise God for the obedience that accompanies your confession of the gospel of Christ, and for your generosity in sharing with them and with everyone else. And in their prayers for you their hearts will go out to you, because of the surpassing grace God has given you. Thanks be to God for his indescribable gift!" (2 Corinthians 9:6–15).

Among the many benefits to working on God's farm is the fruit we are given to enjoy: love, joy, peace, patience, kindness, goodness, faithfulness, gentleness, and self-control (Galatians 5:22). One cool thing about fruit is that the seeds are included. As we enjoy the fruit of the Spirit, seeds are carried everywhere we go. Just the same as when we dispose of an apple core with its seeds, we may not always know where they land when we toss them, and we may not always see what grows, but God promises to send workers to tend to them. "Let us not become weary in doing good, for at the proper time we will reap a harvest if we do not give up" (Galatians 6:9).

Lord Jesus, you said, "The harvest is plentiful but the workers are few ... therefore, send out workers into your harvest field." Send me up to your farm. I love to work for you! Amen.

18. Sowing and Reaping

If you plant strawberries, you get _____? If you plant peas, you get _____? If you plant marigolds, you get _____? In the natural, these would be "duh" questions, right? Even though seed is sown underground and the roots take hold in dark places, what we plant is eventually revealed obviously to the rest of the world as the crop comes in—we reap what we sow.

"The acts of the sinful nature are obvious: sexual immorality, impurity and debauchery; idolatry and witchcraft; hatred, discord, jealousy, fits of rage, selfish ambition, dissentions, factions and envy; drunkenness, orgies, and the like. I warn you, as I did before, that those who live like this will not inherit the kingdom of God. But the fruit of the Spirit is love, joy, peace, patience, kindness, goodness, faithfulness, gentleness and self-control. Against such things there is no law" (Galatians 5:19–23). "Do not be deceived: God cannot be mocked. A man reaps what he sows. The one who sows to please his sinful nature will reap destruction; the one who sows to please the Spirit, from the Spirit will reap eternal life. Let us not grow weary in doing good, for at the proper time we will reap a harvest if we do not give up. Therefore, as we have opportunity, let us do good to all people, especially to those who belong to the family of believers" (Galatians 6:7–9). We are often given this concept, the "law of reciprocity," as a warning: Beware, you reap what you sow, and that is the truth, but it is the flip side of a very great promise: The good you do will return to you as blessings!

I repeat the same principle as it applies to giving: "Remember this: Whoever sows sparingly will also reap sparingly, and whoever sows generously will also reap generously. Each man should give what he has decided in his heart to give, not reluctantly or under compulsion, for God loves a cheerful giver. And God is able to make all grace abound to you, so that in all things at all times, having all that you need, you will abound in every good work. As it is written: 'He has scattered abroad his gifts to the poor; his righteousness endures forever'" (2 Corinthians 9:6–9).

Seed to sow is placed at our disposal. Sowing it is up to us; the time of the harvest is up to God, and we must not give up tending the field until God's time arrives. Remember that patience is a fruit of the Spirit. No crop comes in the day it is sown, except by a miracle, and yes, he still does miracles, but "be patient, then, brothers, until the Lord's coming. See how the farmer waits for the land to yield its valuable crop and how patient he is for the autumn and spring rains. You, too, be patient and stand firm, because the Lord's coming is near" (James 5:7–8).

Lord of the harvest, I ask for good seed to sow in the ground you appoint, and for the rain and sun and the rich soil to nourish that seed. Help me to be a faithful steward of the seed you have assigned to me until the harvest comes in, for your kingdom's sake. Amen.

19. Patience

Perhaps this is a good place to focus for a moment on patience. "As the rain and the snow come down from heaven, and do not return to it without watering the earth and making it bud and flourish, so that it yields seed for the sower and bread for the eater, so is my word that goes out from my mouth: it will not return to me empty, but will accomplish what I desire and achieve the purpose for which I sent it," says the Lord in Isaiah 55:10–11. The rain comes to minister to the earth so it will produce. Snow also comes to water the earth. Picture a snow-capped mountain. That snow up there on top doesn't do a whole lot of watering until the air at its altitude warms up and melts it. Then it trickles down the mountain to feed streams and rivers that water the thirsty land. The provision is sent in one season, but is not visible until another season. The preceding verses in Isaiah say, "'For my thoughts are not your thoughts, neither are your ways my ways,' declares the Lord. 'As the heavens are higher than the earth, so are my ways higher than your ways and my thoughts higher than your thoughts'" (8–9). The Lord knows the time and place the blessing will be needed, and he arranges things so it will arrive right on time!

"There is a time for everything, and a season for every activity under heaven" (Ecclesiastes 3:1). There is no promise that there will be a season of fruit every single day. God, who knows the end from the beginning, has our best interest at heart. There come times when we endure trials, and sometimes those trials seem like they will never end, and we tend to cry out, "Why, God?" My young friend Tiffany gives a good word: "If we are going to ask 'Why me?'

in the hard times, we must also ask 'Why me?' in the good times, for we have done nothing to merit the favor of God, even though he has opened the door of heaven for us." The key is to never give up hope. Because God calls the times and seasons, he will always bring forth the proper crop in the proper season. "Blessed is the man who does not walk in the counsel of the wicked or stand in the way of sinners or sit in the seat of mockers [even when doing those things might seem to bring about the desired results more quickly]. But his delight is in the law of the Lord, and on that law he meditates day and night. He is like a tree planted by the rivers of water that yields its fruit in season, and whose leaf does not wither" (Psalm 1:1–3).

The most devastating mistakes—life altering mistakes—I have ever made in my life are the times when I decided that God was just not moving fast enough, that he must need my help to bring about his promises in my life. After all, he is pretty busy. Maybe he forgot. I'll just take this little step on my own ... You know the drill. Abraham did it, too, when he waited so long for the coming of the promised son and he and Sarah decided to give God a little help. Look at the news; that war is still being fought.

"Be patient, then, brothers, until the Lord's coming. See how the farmer waits for the land to yield its valuable crop and how patient he is for the autumn and spring rains (James 5:7). When it comes right down to it, there's really nothing the farmer can do but wait and be patient for the right time. He can add nutrients to the soil; he can weed and hoe and pamper the plants, but until the time is right, the crops don't come. Yes, patience is a fruit of the Spirit, and we can have confidence that we wait for the one who holds all things in his hands.

Holy God, omnipotent, omniscient, and omnipresent, I trust in you. Keep my seasons turning as they should, and help me to wait for you. Amen

The Hard Stuff

20. The Creation's Creation

Several years ago, my daughter and I went to see a stage production of *The Phantom of the Opera*. It had been a favorite book of ours, and we had enjoyed the film version together at the theater and on DVD. We had excellent seats and the musicians and actors were outstanding, but as much as I thoroughly enjoyed it, the images I was seeing on the stage were just not the film actors I had accepted as "Erik" and "Christine" in my mind. The stage production seemed to me to be a nice *imitation*. Well, OK, I realize that theater is all just an imitation of life, but that lesson sort of revealed the way it is with idols. We get a mental image of what God should be, and we construct him according to our mental image.

Another example might be those generic products at the store. Whether it's crackers or sodas or cereals, the generic brands just don't seem quite the same after the original. That's the way it is with God—any representation we might formulate, regardless of our motives, limits him to a human idea, human craft, and human manipulation. To venerate any representation of God—statue, crucifix, picture, etc.—is to limit God to a cheap imitation, a generic substitute, the creation's creation.

I don't think God has anything against artistic renderings as long as they are kept in perspective. He, himself, commissioned the sculpting and weaving of cherubim, angels, trees, flowers and fruit for the adornment of his tabernacle. The concern arises in Exodus 20:5 which says, "You shall not bow down to them or worship them; for I, the Lord your God, am a jealous God." The natural mind of man desires something tangible to which he can relate *naturally*, but the reality is that God is not *natural*, he is *supernatural*; he is *spirit*. In the words of Jesus, "God is spirit, and his worshipers must worship in spirit and in truth" (John 4:24).

A problem with idols, whether physical or mental, is addressed by G. K. Beale in his book *We Become What We Worship*. "You eventually become like your idol. We have created idols after our own image. And that's exactly what we try to do with God, but we don't do it physically with wood or stone, but in a mental way." It's not hard to see this principle at work. Our children "idolize" the latest rock star, athlete, or actor. They not only want to dress like them and fix their hair in similar fashions, but they emulate their speech, imitate their walk, adopt their habits, anything to be like them. The Bible tells us to "offer your bodies as living sacrifices, holy and pleasing to God—this is your spiritual act of worship. Do not conform any longer to the pattern of this world, but be transformed by the renewing of your mind" (Romans 12:1–2). The emphasis is on what is unseen over what is seen, the spiritual over the carnal, the godly over the worldly.

There are some privileges that God has reserved for himself alone. Perhaps he did not want images of himself created by people because it was his plan to do that himself. Jesus asked, "Don't you know me, Philip, even after I have been among you such a long time? Anyone who has seen me has seen the Father. How can you say, 'Show us the Father'? Don't you believe that I am in the Father and that the Father is in me? The words I say to you are not just my own. Rather, it is the Father, living in me, who is doing his work" (John 14:9–10).

The image of the Father revealed through the Son, Jesus Christ, is the image to which we should seek to conform. It's not a work that can be accomplished by the hands of man, but only by the will of God and the work of the Holy Spirit. In Romans 12:2, we are told to be *transformed*. This is the same Greek word from which we derive the English word *metamorphosis*. It is not instantaneous;

it is a process, like the life of a butterfly. If we are willing to invest in the transformation, Jesus is, too. In fact, he has already done so: "You are not your own; you were bought at a price" (1 Corinthians 6:19b–20a).

Lord, help me not to make idols or worship the creation's creation, but shape me into your image and likeness in order to best serve you. Amen.

21. Paths

I received an email from an acquaintance one day. The title was a little strange and seductive, so I ignored it. I went back to it later, and started to click on it twice, but decided against it. Curiosity killed the cat, right? Even though I thought this was a person I could trust not to send any ungodly material, something just didn't seem right.

Sin, even sin that we believe is overcome in our lives, can try to raise its ugly head over and over again. And sin is addictive. Just like an alcoholic who has stopped drinking should never reach for that "only one drink" again, we should not let sin get even a toenail in the door. Illegal drugs, cigarettes, pornography, and stealing, for sure, can overcome our self-control if we are not careful, but what about over-eating, using the Lord's name irreverently, gossiping, lying? And what about the invisible things: envy, hatred, pride, lust, or meditating on things that don't glorify God? We all struggle with something.

Let me emphasize something: *the struggle is not the sin!* Without a battle, there can be no victory. Sin comes when we give in to that thing that we know is not of God, and once we have given in, it is far too easy to keep giving in until we develop spiritual callouses that can no longer feel the damage that is being done. "Be self-controlled and alert. Your enemy the devil prowls around like a roaring lion seeking whom he may devour. Resist him" (1 Peter 5:8–9a).

I didn't click on the email message, and later found out that it was a trap, not sent by the person I know, but by someone who had attached a virus to it and sent it out over the internet. "For a man's ways are in full view of the Lord, and he examines all his paths" (Proverbs 5:21).

Lord, guide me in the paths you would have me walk, and keep me from sin. Amen.

22. RSVP

"First John" is a letter written to believers, those who have already accepted Jesus Christ as Lord and Savior, written by the apostle John, son of Zebedee, fisherman, author, prophet and friend of Jesus. Those are pretty impressive credentials! "I write these things to you who believe in the name of the Son of God, so that you may know that you have eternal life. This is the confidence we have in approaching God: that if we ask anything according to his will, he hears us. And if we know that he hears us—whatever we ask—we know that we have what we asked of him" (1 John 5:13–15).

It never ceases to amaze me how people, even some who call themselves Christians, criticize God for not answering prayers. Often, they are the ones who claim his name, but have no relationship with him. If there is no relationship, no prayer, no scripture reading, no communication, one cannot know how to ask anything "according to his will," because he doesn't know what his will is. I could call myself a Walton all month long, but I doubt the bank would be too impressed if I tried to write a check in that name. Although I frequent their establishments on a regular basis, I have no relationship with them. I remember hearing a famous evangelist say, "It's impertinent to ask God for things when you don't even know him." The epistle also says, "If we claim to have fellowship with him, yet walk in darkness, we lie and do not live by the truth. But if we walk in light, as he is in the light, we have fellowship with one another, and the blood of Jesus, his Son purifies us from all sin" (1:6–7).

It is unfortunate, but important, to realize that everyone is not an heir to God's promises. His promises and sonship are *offered* to all, but we have to come to God on his terms, and his terms are based on our response to his Son. Our right relationship with God, according to John's letters, means that we understand that we are sinners in need of grace, and that we recognize and receive the grace that comes through Christ alone. On this side of heaven, we will never be perfect, "but if anybody does sin, we have one who speaks to the Father in our defense—Jesus Christ, the righteous one. He is the atoning sacrifice for our sins" (2:1b–2a).

A right relationship with God also means that we walk in love. "Dear friends, let us love one another, for love comes from God. Everyone who loves has been born of God and knows God. Whoever does not love does not know God, because God is love" (1 John 4:7–8). We were created in the image and likeness of God and he loves all the people of the world unconditionally, but unconditional love does not mean unconditional promises. Look at John 3:16: "For God so loved the world that he gave his one and only Son (unconditional love), that whoever believes in him shall not perish, but have eternal life (conditional promise). Jesus said, "I am the way and the truth and the life; no one comes to the Father except through me" (John 14:6).

I remember a heart-breaking conclusion to a discussion that I had with some friends once, that the only sadness in heaven will be God's sadness over those who did not repent and accept the blood of Jesus. Since there are no tears in heaven, we probably won't even remember those who we were close to in this life who didn't receive Christ, because how could we not grieve for our loved ones who are forever lost? But God will remember them, his beloved, and his heart will be forever broken over those who refused his invitation. That is not scripture, but I think it is true.

The invitation has been written and sent to all, signed in his blood. It is up to us to RSVP—yes, Lord, I come!

23. Hypocrisy

How many times have you heard someone use the word *hypocrisy* as an excuse for not attending church? "Those places are just full of hypocrites! They act one way in church and another way everywhere else. They aren't any better than me"—you know the drill. Hypocrisy is no new problem in man's relationship with God.

The prophet Jeremiah lamented to God, "You have planted them and they have taken root; they grow and bear fruit. You are always on their lips but far from their hearts" (12:2). Isaiah wrote, "The Lord says: 'These people come near to me with their mouth, and honor me with their lips, but their hearts are far from me. Their worship of me is made up only of rules taught by men'" (29:13–14). Jesus quoted those very words when he addressed the Pharisees in Matthew 15, the group he referred to as hypocrites by name in Matthew 23. The word *hypocrite* as he used it literally translates as an actor assuming a character part. The Pharisees were absolutely not what they wished people to believe they were, and they used their office to control and manipulate the people who truly desired to follow God.

The fact that Jesus pointed out the problem did not make it go away. The epistles are full of accusation. "To the pure all things are pure, but to those who are corrupted and do not believe, nothing is pure. In fact, both their minds and their consciences are corrupted. They claim to know God, but by their actions they deny him. They are detestable, disobedient and unfit for anything good" (Titus 1:15–16). Timothy said to have nothing to do with those "having a form of godliness but denying its power" (2 Timothy 2:5). According to 1 John 2:4, "The man who says, 'I know him,' but does not do what he says is a liar, and the truth is not in him." Hypocrisy causes all sorts of problems, and not only in the church. Remember the law of reciprocity? We reap what we sow.

Before we get too comfortable in our own righteousness (But Lord, *I'm* not a hypocrite!), let's consider the words of Paul: "We know that the law is spiritual; but I am unspiritual, sold as a slave to sin. I do not understand what I do. For what I want to do I do not do, but what I hate, I do. And if I do what I do not want to do, I agree that the law is good. As it is, it is no longer I myself who do it, but it is sin living in me. I know that nothing good lives in me, that is, my sinful nature. For I have the desire to do what is good, but I cannot carry it out. For what I do is not the good I want to do; no, the evil I do not want to do—this I keep on doing. Now if I do what I do not want to do, it is no longer I who do it, but it is sin living in me that does it. So I find this law at work: When I want to do good, evil is right there with me. For in my inner being I delight in God's law; but I see another law at work in the members of my body, waging war against the law of my mind and making me a prisoner of the law of sin at work within my members. What a wretched man I am! Who will rescue me from this body of death?" (Romans 7:14–24). This comes from the man who penned twelve books of the New Testament!

My advice: If someone calls you a hypocrite because you attend church, say, "Yes, you are absolutely right. I am a sinner saved by grace, and, praise God, I am a work in progress." Let's face it, we all have our issues, and we will as long as we're in this flesh, try as we may. "Therefore, I urge you, brothers, in view of God's mercy, to offer your bodies as living sacrifices, holy and pleasing to God—this is our spiritual act of worship. Do not conform any longer to the pattern of this world, but be transformed by the renewing of your mind. Then you will be able to test and approve what God's will is—his good, pleasing and perfect will (Romans 12:1–2). One great thing here is the word *transformed*. As I mentioned before, it comes from the Greek word from which we derive the English word *metamorphosis*, like the caterpillar to butterfly scenario. Our transformation is not instantaneous, but a process. If we seem, from time to time, hypocritical during the process (and we will), we are comforted by the fact that God is not finished with us yet. Cliché, yes; fact, also yes.

Now for those who don't attend church because of the hypocrisy they might encounter there, you might ask them if they go to work ... or the store ... or the movies—any hypocrites there?

Heavenly Father, gracious Lord, please forgive me for my hypocrisy. I ask that you deliver me from my sinful nature and help me to become more like you, transformed by the renewing of my mind, not so I can seem better than others or feel better than others, but so I may be a more effective worker in your kingdom. Thank you for never giving up on me! Amen.

24. Fights

Do Christians fight? Uhhhh … yes, and the arguments and conflicts are not always with non-Christians. Unfortunately, since we are inhabitants of this evil age, we sometimes desire to passionately defend ourselves or to seek revenge. In a school where I once worked, the "Matthew 18 Principle" was part of the contract we had to sign each year. It goes like this:

"If your brother sins against you, go and show him his fault, just between the two of you. If he listens to you, you have won your brother over. But if he will not listen, take one or two others along, so that every matter may be established by the testimony of two or three witnesses. If he refuses to listen to them, tell it to the church, and if he refuses to listen even to the church, treat him as you would a pagan or a tax collector [that is, separate yourself from him]" (15–17).

Our first instruction is to seek reconciliation and forgiveness. Many times in the scriptures, God voices his desire for unity. See how closely these verses are followed by the parable of the unforgiving servant, who after begging before the king and having his great debt canceled, went out and found his fellow servant who owed him a comparatively small debt. "His fellow servant fell to his knees and begged him, 'Be patient with me, and I will pay you back.' But he refused. Instead, he went off and had the man thrown into prison until he could pay the debt. When the other servants saw what had happened, they were greatly distressed and went and told their master everything that had happened. Then the master called the servant in. 'You wicked servant,' he said. 'I canceled all that debt of yours because you begged me to. Shouldn't you have had mercy on your fellow servant just as I had on you?' In anger his master turned him over to the jailers to be tortured, until he should pay back all he owed" (23–34).

Obviously, we should approach every situation in the love of Christ who reveals that we do not struggle against our fellow servant, "but against the rulers, against the authorities, against the powers of this dark world and against spiritual forces of evil in heavenly realms" (Ephesians 6:12). We must remember that the enemy of mankind takes no joy in the unity of the Church, and if he can stir up trouble in it, he will do it. His plans are often subtle and infiltrate the community church: someone took offense at a reference in a sermon, the church foyer was painted an ugly color, the offering money was not used the way someone thought it should be, the restrooms didn't get cleaned, etc. Jesus said, "Every kingdom divided against itself will be ruined, and every city or household divided against itself will not stand" (Matthew 12:25). Our enemy often aims his attacks against our families and against our church families. It is important to understand that our public show of anger, our gossip and back-biting, our caustic criticism can discredit our church, our pastor who is the shepherd over us, and even our Lord, in the eyes of the world, and can dishearten those who are young in the faith. The world always seems to look for reasons to criticize the Body of Christ, so we need to take care not to provide those reasons.

Although, hopefully, it does not arise often, there do come occasions when we need to separate ourselves from someone, and there is a biblical precedent for that. "Some time later Paul said to Barnabas, 'Let us go back and visit the brothers in all the towns where we preached the word of the Lord and see how they are doing.' Barnabas wanted to take John, also called Mark, with them, but Paul did not think it wise to take him because he had deserted them in Pamphylia and had not continued with them in the work. They had such a *sharp disagreement* that they parted company. Barnabas took Mark and sailed for Cyprus, but Paul chose Silas and left, commended by the brothers to the grace of the Lord. He went through Cyria and Cicilia, strengthening the churches" (Acts 15:36–41).

The Bible says they had a "sharp disagreement," a fight, yet they did not waste time in revenge or feuds. Their work continued, and even more so because the Word of God was carried in two directions instead of one. A public fight and unforgiveness would have damaged the ministry, because others would have observed that they did not practice the love of Christ that they preached. Their arrangement, in spite of their differences, ensured that the church was not damaged. They also did not spread evil report about one another, and were eventually reconciled (see 1 Corinthians 9:6, Galatians 2:11–13, 1 Peter 5:13, Colossians 4:10, 2 Timothy 4:11).

I heard it said once that the closer we walk to one another, the more likely we are to bump into each other. Quarrels and disagreements arise even within the body of Christ. How we handle those quarrels reveals our hearts and our willingness to truly be "transformed by the renewing of our minds" into the image of Christ who has "called us out of darkness and into his marvelous light."

Lord Jesus, I confess my anger and my pride and my desire to see others punished when I feel I have been wronged. I confess my judgmental attitudes. Thank you for your patience and for not giving up on me. Help me daily to conform more and more into your image of humility and forgiveness, and to seek peace and pursue it with all my brothers and sisters—the great, diverse, multi-cultural, multi-talented Body of Christ. Amen.

25. A Word About Gossip

This lesson is very personal to me and was a revelation at a very critical moment in my life. I was working in a supervisory position—three years as a program director taught me one thing, administration is *not* my spiritual gift—and I was having some problems with a couple of my employees. My personal life was also in a turmoil. My daughter was five years old at the time. One morning she came into my bedroom and told me, "Last night there was something in the hall, and it tried to come into my room and it tried to go into Joey's room and it tried to go into your room, but the angels wouldn't let it, and its name was *Sorcery*." That was a very chilling moment. My five-year-old had heard of angels, but as far as I could figure, *sorcery* had never been a part of her experience or vocabulary. It drove me to my knees and to my Bible.

The Holy Spirit led me first to Psalm 8:2: "From the lips of children and infants you have ordained praise because of your enemies, to silence the foe and the avenger." The first part of this verse is quoted often, but I wonder how many consider the second part. I had never paid it any attention before. Consulting my concordance and lexicon I found that *foe* literally translated was an enemy, an opponent, or someone from another tribe, and that *avenger* was literally someone holding a grudge and seeking punishment for someone else. It sounded to me when I first read the verse that *foe* and *avenger* were a single entity, but by definition, they seemed to be two separate entities working together for no good. I remembered the scriptures about the power in agreement: "Again, I tell you that if two of you on earth agree about anything you ask for, it will be done for you by my Father in heaven. For where two or three come together in my name, there am I with them" (Matthew 18:19–20); "Calling the Twelve to him, he sent them two by two and gave them authority over evil spirits (Mark 6:7); "After this, the Lord appointed seventy-two others and sent them two by two ahead of him into every town and place he was about to go (Luke 10:1). It occurred to me that there was a basic spiritual truth here, that there is power in agreement, whether that be ordained by God or by the enemy of our souls. I also studied the word *sorcery*, and found something that made the puzzle begin to come together. One Old Testament root of the word *sorcery* is "to whisper." The truth hit me like a ton of bricks! Whispering is a way to cloak gossip, and the gossip of those unhappy employees had (hopefully unintentionally) partnered them with the spirit of darkness who hates every child of God. Because of my weakened spiritual condition due to the stressful circumstances in my life, my armor was not in place, and I was a target. I immediately contacted a few people I knew who were prayer warriors, and together we prayed against the power of the gossip, and the adversary's hold was broken!

Remember what James says: "Consider what a great forest is set on fire by a small spark. The tongue also is a fire, a world of evil among the parts of the body. It corrupts the whole person, sets the whole course of his life on fire, and is itself set on fire by hell ... It is a restless evil, full of deadly poison" (3:5b–6, 8b). "But if you harbor bitter envy and selfish ambition in your hearts, do not boast about it or deny the truth. Such 'wisdom' does not come down from heaven but is earthly, unspiritual, of the devil. For where you have envy and selfish ambition, there you find disorder and every evil practice. But the wisdom that comes from heaven is first of all pure; then peace-loving, considerate, submissive, full of mercy and good fruit, impartial and sincere. Peacemakers who sow in peace will raise a harvest of righteousness" (14–18).

Please don't get me wrong. We all have problems with the tongue, but the warnings from scripture are clear, and we should guard ourselves against being used by the enemy as well as being attacked by the enemy. Second Corinthians 12:20 lists gossip along with quarreling, jealousy, anger, factions, slander, arrogance and disorder. Consider these verses from Proverbs: "A perverse man stirs up dissension, and a gossip separates close friends" (16:28), "The words of a gossip are like choice morsels; they go down to a man's innermost parts" (18:8), "A gossip betrays a confidence, so avoid a man who talks too much" (20:19), "Without wood a fire goes out; without gossip a quarrel dies down. As charcoal to embers and as wood to fire, so is a quarrelsome man for kindling strife" (26:20–21). And we can't hide our gossip by the disclaimer, "I'm only telling you this because I know you'll pray about it" (ouch!) because Proverbs also says, "A malicious man disguises himself with his lips, but in his heart he harbors deceit. Though his speech is charming, do not believe him, for seven abominations fill his heart. His malice may be concealed by deception, but his wickedness will be exposed in the assembly" (26:24–26).

We live in an evil age, and many people, even those who call themselves Christians, are seduced into evil practices, but we are not without hope. Jesus prayed for his disciples saying, "My prayer is not that you take them out of the world but that you protect them from the evil one. They are not of the world, even as I am not of it. Sanctify them by the truth; your word is truth. As you have sent me into the world, I have sent them into the world. For them I sanctify myself, that they too may be truly sanctified" (John 17:15–19).

Holy Lord Jesus, touch my lips with a coal from the altar of heaven; sanctify me; let my words glorify you, and guard me from the wiles of the enemy. Amen.

26. Unattractive

This is hard to write. I suppose it is a confession. I ask pardon in advance from anyone I may offend; no offense is intended. Please grant me grace.

One evening several years ago as Christmas was approaching, I was racing into Walmart to grab a few last-minute items. As I neared the entrance, I noticed a man in a wheelchair almost blocking my path. He had only one leg and part of one of his hands was missing. He was incredibly ragged and when I got close I could smell him. He was begging for money. My reaction—discomfort, embarrassment and *repulsion*. I wish I could put that word in a smaller font. Even if he had been clean and in the church foyer, I think I still would have tried to avoid him, because I just never knew how to respond to people with such extreme physical challenges. I walked within feet of him, smiled without making eye contact, voiced a weak "hello," and quickened my pace until I was safely inside the store thinking, "Maybe he'll be gone by the time I come out."

I was in the middle of the frozen food section (ironically) when I was hit by such shame and conviction that tears came to my eyes. I was so blessed. I had a wonderful, healthy family, good personal health, a beautiful, clean home, and I was heading that evening to a party with dear loving friends—things he obviously did not have. How could I be harboring such a frozen heart? I didn't have much cash with me, so I quickly put a few items back praying, "Lord, let him still be there when I get back!" I paid for my items, got my change and raced out the door. There he was! I walked over to him and handed him the money, and then Jesus took over!

"Do you know Jesus, Sir?"

"Yes, Ma'am."

"Do you know how much he loves you?"

No answer, just tears.

"May I pray with you?"

"Yes."

I knelt by this man and took hold of his mutilated hands, and prayed for him gently, that his heart would be overwhelmed by the love of his heavenly Father, and then I hugged him. The funny thing is, I don't think I prayed for him so much because *he* needed it (although we can all use the prayer and encouragement of another) as because *I* needed it. I needed to learn to love more like Jesus and to recognize the hurt of others through his eyes. You see, the thing that convicted me in the frozen food section was that God gave me just a glimpse of the way I looked to him before I asked Jesus into my heart. I was ragged, filthy, stinking to high heaven, and so incomplete, much worse off than that man at the door. How could I *not* reach out to a fellow human soul after what Jesus had done for me?

There was a time when Jesus was unattractive. He stumbled to Calvary bloody, sweaty, feverish, dirty, and abused. "He had no beauty or majesty to attract us to him, nothing in his appearance that we should desire him. He was despised and rejected by men, a man of sorrows and familiar with suffering. Like one from whom men hide their faces he was despised, and we esteemed him not" (Isaiah 53:2b–3). Would I have loved that Jesus if I had seen him for the first time that day? Would I have reached out to the one who was crushed so that I could gain heaven? I'm afraid of my answer.

Lord, I am so humbly grateful for the lessons you continue to teach. Thank you for becoming unattractive and despised so that I can be clean and loved. Help me to receive all who you send to me, whatever their condition, and to see them through your eyes. Help me to love as you love. Amen.

Before I Go . . .

27. Don't Forget the TP

In my home, I usually do the shopping. I go faithfully every week, and because at my house we love to cook and we love to eat, I usually end up with a pretty full cart at the check-out. I don't do a bad job, but there is one thing I can never seem to remember—toilet paper! I *always* forget the toilet paper! And believe me, this is not something that goes unnoticed!

One of the fundamentals of our rather spoiled society, we always know immediately when we run out of toilet paper, and it is a very uncomfortable situation. It's hard to determine the proper course of action in those moments when you realize, it's just not there. I'm certainly not going to make any suggestions here.

It's hard on my ego, too, because no matter what other wonderful items I buy, it's the toilet paper that's going to be missed. I can remember the chicken, the pork chops, several kinds and cuts of cheese, bread, tea, coffee, chocolate (not likely to forget that), and even the good-for-you stuff like milk, apples, and eggs, but all of those have a substitute in case they're missing. We can even use baking soda if I forget tooth paste. But what can one substitute for toilet paper? The facial tissues don't last long and the paper towels are rough and clog things up—there's just no good option. There's always the nearest "rippy mart," but they never have the right brand and it's always more expensive; and besides, when you realize the need, you are already "in the moment," so to speak.

I'm really going to try to commit myself to remembering from now on. After all, it's not like the day is going to come when we'll get tired of toilet paper or stop needing it, at least not on this side of the grave. Maybe I'll just begin buying in quantity. A big supply could be a good thing.

So, what's my point? First John 3:11 says we should love one another. The Scriptures also teach: "Better a meal of vegetables where there is love than a fattened calf with hatred" (Proverbs 15:17); "Let no debt remain outstanding except the continuing debt to love one another, for he who loves his fellow man is fulfilling the law" (Romans 13:8); "Many waters cannot quench love; rivers cannot wash it away. If one were to give all the wealth of the house for love, it would not be enough" (Song of Solomon 8:7); "If I speak in the tongues of men and of angels, but have not love, I am only a resounding gong or a clanging cymbal. If I have the gift of prophecy and can fathom all mysteries and all knowledge, and if I have the faith that can move mountains, but have not love, I am nothing. If I give all I have to the poor and surrender my body to the flames, but have not love, I gain nothing" (1 Corinthians 13:1–3); "Dear friends, let us love one another, for love comes from God. Everyone who loves has been born of God and knows God. Whoever does not love does not know God, because God is love" (1 John 4:7–8).

Am I trying to say that love and toilet paper are the same? Well, they're hard to do without, you always know when they're missing; no matter what other great things you have, they can't take their place, there is no substitute for the right kind, and the need for them is not going to go away.

Lord, whatever else I may forget today, help me not to forget to love.

28. Love Your Neighbor

The Hebrew word *Leviticus* literally translates into English as "and the Lord called." The book lays down the laws for worship, ceremony, and holiness as they were given through Moses. Levitical laws included, among many things, the instructions for sacrifice. Although we may consider it a New Testament concept, the Israelites were called to sacrifice their pride as well as their animals. "Do not seek revenge or bear a grudge against one of your people, but love your neighbor as yourself: I am the Lord" (Leviticus 19:18), could be paraphrased, "Sacrifice your pride. Put to death whatever anger or grudges you hold against another. Choose to love instead, because that's what I do, and I am your God."

As much as Old Testament law is now fulfilled by grace, this admonition continues in its pure form throughout the New Testament. It expresses the character of God, who loves us all. Jesus said it (Matthew 22:39, Mark 12:31, Luke 10:27), Paul said it (Romans 13:9, Galatians 5:14), and James said it (James 2:8).

Anger and vengeance will break the back of the one who carries it. Jesus' "yoke is easy and his burden is light." Jesus said, "Love the Lord your God with all your heart and with all your soul and with all your mind. This is the first and greatest commandment. And the second is like it: Love your neighbor as yourself. All the law and prophets hang on these two commandments" (Matthew 22:37–40).

Jesus, my Lord and Savior, you forgave all my trespasses. Help me to nail my pride to the cross and to never hold a grudge or plot revenge against my neighbor who is made in your image. Thank you for the freedom that comes with forgiveness. Amen.

29. The Greatest of These

"And now these three remain: faith, hope and love. But the greatest of these is love" (1 Corinthians 13:13). Ever wonder, why love? Why is love greater than faith? Why is love greater than hope? "Through [Jesus Christ] we have gained access by *faith* into this grace in which we stand, and we rejoice in the *hope* of the glory of God. Not only so, but we also rejoice in our sufferings, because we know that suffering produces perseverance; perseverance, character, and character, *hope*. And *hope* does not disappoint us, because God has poured out his love into our hearts by the Holy Spirit whom he has given to us" (Romans 5:2–5); "In him we were also chosen having been predestined according to the plan of him who works out everything in conformity with the purpose of his will, in order that we, who were the first to put our *hope* in Christ, might be for the praise of his glory. And you also were included in Christ when you heard the word of truth, the gospel of your salvation. Having believed, you were marked in him with a seal, the promised Holy Spirit, who is a deposit guaranteeing our inheritance until the redemption of those who are God's possession—to the praise of his glory" (Ephesians 1:11–14); "Without *faith* it is impossible to please God" (Hebrews 11:6a).

Why is love greater than that? To answer, let me return to an old story: "How you have fallen from heaven, O morning star, son of the dawn! You have been cast down to earth, you who once laid low the nations! You said in your heart, 'I will ascend to heaven; I will raise my throne above the stars of God; I will sit enthroned on the mount of assembly, on the utmost heights of the sacred mountain. I will ascend above the tops of the clouds; I will make myself like the Most High.' But you are brought down to the grave, to the depths of the pit" (Isaiah 14:12–15). The verses tell of the rebellion and fall of Satan. His *pride* got him evicted from heaven. "[Jesus] replied, 'I saw Satan fall like lightning from heaven'" (Luke 10:18).

When Satan approached Eve in the garden, he planted the seed of pride in her as he tempted her with the forbidden fruit. "'You will not surely die [if you eat the fruit],' the serpent said to the woman. 'For God knows that when you eat of it your eyes will be opened and you will be like God, knowing good from evil'" (Genesis 3:4). *Pride* led to the first sin, and *pride* led to the fall of humanity.

Every sin, any sin one can name, now finds its roots in pride. The scriptures warn against pride: "When pride comes, then comes disgrace, but with humility comes wisdom" (Proverbs 11:2); "Pride goes before destruction, a haughty spirit before a fall" (Proverbs 16:18); "Before his downfall a man's heart is proud, but humility comes before honor" (Proverbs 18:12); "But God gives us more grace. That is why the scripture says, 'God opposes the proud but gives grace to the humble'" (James 4:6).

It seems that *humility* should be the opposite of pride, but watch 1 Corinthians 13 where we are told, "Love is patient, love is kind. It does not boast, it is not proud. It is not rude, it is not self-seeking, it is not easily angered. It keeps no record of wrongs, but rejoices in the truth" (4–6). Boastful, self-seeking, angry, remembering others' wrongs, delighting in evil—that is pride. Pride's focus is always on "me." The verses also tell us what is *not* pride—love. If what is not love is pride, and what is not pride is love, then love is the opposite of pride. Pride focuses inward on *me*; love focuses outward on *others*. We might then say that if love is the opposite of pride, and pride is the root of all sin, love is also the opposite of sin. Love is *anti-sin*! And that is why it is the greatest gift. It is the gift that frees the giver from sin. It is the gift that demonstrates the character of God to and in his creation, as we read in 1 John 4:7–8.

It is because of his great love for us that Jesus Christ came into the world and suffered and died and defeated sin, so that we, his beloved, could live with him forever. "For God so loved the world, that he gave his one and only Son, that whoever believes in him shall not perish, but have eternal life" (John 3:16). Hallelujah to the Lamb!

Lord, Jesus, please turn my focus outward, and teach me to love others as you have loved me. Amen.

30. Just Believe

It's amazing how complicated we make things after God has gone out of his way to make them so simple. "Whoever believes in him is not condemned, but whoever does not believe stands condemned already, because he has not believed in the name of the only Son of God" (John 3:18). The equation: No belief = condemnation; Belief = no condemnation. Simple! And I don't do math!

"The word is near you; it is in your mouth and in your heart, that is, the word of faith we are proclaiming: that if you confess with your mouth, 'Jesus is Lord,' and believe in your heart that God raised him from the dead, you will be saved. For it is with your heart that you believe and are justified, and it is with your mouth that you confess and are saved. As the scripture says, 'Anyone who trusts in him will never be put to shame'" (Romans 10:8b–11).

When the Israelites were traveling in the wilderness, they began to complain and doubt God who brought them out of Egypt. They were even discontent with the manna from heaven that God provided miraculously for them. So the Lord sent poisonous snakes that bit the people and caused many of them to die. As they tended to do, the people went to Moses and expressed sorrow for their sins, and Moses prayed for them. "The Lord said to Moses, 'Make a snake and put it up on a pole; anyone who is bitten can look at it and live'" (Numbers 21:8). They only had to *look*. I wonder how many of the Israelites were bitten, but decided it was foolishness to look at a fake snake and died. In the words of someone I used to know, I wonder how many people today are "snake-bit." Jesus taught Nicodemus, "Just as Moses lifted up the snake in the desert, so the Son of Man must be lifted up, that everyone who believes in him may have eternal life" (John 3:14–15).

Unfortunately, as I said before, we are often taught not to believe in what we cannot experience with our five physical senses. But remember the bumble bee. According to the science of aerodynamics, the bumble bee should not be able to accomplish flight, but fly he does. The ultra-intelligent among us may bring up the ideas of simplified linear treatment of oscillating aerofoils vs. the effect of dynamic stall (or something like that). I say, God made the bumble bee to fly, and the bumble bee never thought to doubt his power to do so. He believes he can fly, and he does fly. If bumble bees could understand human logic, I wonder how many of them would be walking.

We were created to believe in our Creator, but shedding our twenty-first century human junk can be difficult. In my times of doubt, I choose to pray like the father of the boy in Mark 9. Jesus said, "Everything is possible to him who believes." The man responded, "I do believe; help me overcome my unbelief." My human faith is imperfect, but I know that the perfect will come. Just like I work out my physical muscles to the best of my ability then leave the rest to God, I will work out my spiritual muscles, my faith, to the best of my ability and leave the rest to Christ. He's never let me down.

Jesus, I do believe; help me overcome my unbelief. Amen

31. Don't Just Stand There

Jesus had fulfilled his earthly purpose and prepared to go back to heaven so, as he promised, the Holy Spirit would come. Before he left, he gave a final command: "All authority in heaven and earth has been given to me. Therefore go and make disciples of all nations, baptizing them in the name of the Father and of the Son and of the Holy Spirit, and teaching them to obey everything I have commanded you. And surely, I am with you always, to the very end of the age (Matthew 28:18–20). Luke added, "But you will receive power when the Holy Spirit comes on you, and you will be my witnesses in Jerusalem, and all Judea and Samaria, and to the ends of the earth" (Acts 1:8).

"After he said this, he was taken up before their very eyes, and a cloud hid him from their sight. They were looking intently up into the sky as he was going, when suddenly, two men dressed in white stood beside them. 'Men of Galilee,' they said, 'why do you stand here looking into the sky? This same Jesus, who has been taken from you into heaven, will come back in the same way you have seen him go into heaven'" (Acts 1:10–11).

Jesus gave directions, and what did his disciples do? Stood there! I can almost hear the tone of those men in white. "Don't just stand there! Do something!" The first instruction on the timeline was to go to Jerusalem and wait for the coming of the Holy Spirit. The event came within the next month and a half. In the meantime, the apostles were not idle. They organized, replaced Judas with Matthias, and "they all joined together constantly in prayer" (Acts 1:14). Then came what we call in literature, the inciting moment, the event that kicks off the action. There was the sound of a rushing, mighty wind, tongues of fire rested upon each one of them, and they began to speak in other tongues, Peter preached, and over 3,000 people joined them! It was on!

I tell people often that there is no retirement plan for disciples of Christ. Those of whom we have record got busy and did what Jesus commanded. Simon Peter helped Paul to establish the church in Rome until he was crucified upside-down, according to tradition, feeling himself unworthy to die in the same manner as the Lord. Andrew is said to have gone to Scythia, Greece, Asia Minor, and Thrace before being martyred in Achaia. Philip preached in Phrygia until he died in Hierapolis. Matthew wrote his gospel as he remained in Jerusalem, then went to the Medes and Persians as a missionary before being martyred in Ethiopia. Thomas preached in Parthia until he was killed by a lance. James Alpheus spread the word of Christ until he was thrown from the temple, stoned and killed with a club. James spread his faith in Jesus Christ far and wide, stopping only when he was put to death by Herod Agrippa I. John wrote his gospel and the Book of Revelation. Bartholomew (also called Nathanael) traveled and preached the word of God.

There are many since who have heard the call to "Don't just stand there! Do something!"—Martin Luther, John Calvin, John Wycliffe, Billy Graham, Mother Teresa, William Carey, Mary Slessor, Hudson Taylor, Dietrich Bonhoeffer, David Brainerd, Nate Saint, Jim Elliot, we could go on and on. But the command is to you and me, as well. Those men in white also call out to us, "Don't just stand there! Do something!" "The harvest is plentiful, but the workers are few. Ask the Lord of the harvest, therefore, to send workers into his harvest field. Go!" (Luke 10:1b–3a). We all have work to do, and whether that means leaving the country or just leaving our comfort zone, whether it means intercessory prayer, feeding the hungry, telling co-workers or classmates the Good News, doing a kindness for a neighbor, sending a prophetic word over the internet, or even writing a book, I most heartily encourage you, in the mighty Name of Jesus, "Don't just stand there! Do something!"

Lord Jesus, help me to go out and put into practice all that you have taught me.

And by the way, I look forward to coffee on the porch with you again soon!

Works Cited

Beale, G. K. *We Become What We Worship: A Biblical Theology of Idolatry*. IVP Academic, 2009.

The Holy Bible: King James Version. Nashville: Thomas Nelson, 2010.

The Holy Bible: New International Version, Containing the Old Testament and New Testament. Grand Rapids: Zondervan Bible Publishers, 1978.

Printed in the United States
By Bookmasters